I0626907

A Feast for the Hunger We All Have

A 12-course buffet of poetry

by Kelly Watts Williams

Bonus Content:  *Spoken Word performances by Kelly Watts Williams*

GOLDNOOK PUBLISHING

Copyright © 2025 by Kelly Watts Williams

All rights reserved. No part of this book may be reproduced in any form or by any electronic or mechanical means, including information storage and retrieval systems without prior permission in writing from the author.

First paperback edition March 2025
Second printing, revised July 2025
Contains images created by Kelly Watts Williams
Edited by Marsha Mills
Cover art by Kelly Watts Williams
Layout and Format by Kelly Watts Williams and Marsha Mills
Author Photo by Terri Bhutwala

Published by GoldNook Publishing, Chattanooga
ISBN: 979-8-9910300-2-1
Made in the United States of America.

Acknowledgements

I would like to thank the Social and Public Art Resource Center (SPARC) and Dr. Judith Baca, for allowing me to use photos of the Great Wall of Los Angeles. Judy's friendship and support of my artistic journey is much appreciated.

Thanks to all the friends and family who have listened, read, and provided feedback on the various drafts of my poetry and art. So many folks have helped me in my journey to publishing this first book, to name a few: Kathie, Shelia, Kent, Kasey, Derek, Andrea, Vickie, Terri, and Tara.

A special thanks to Rhyme N Chatt Interactive Poetry Organization for its commitment to providing poets a space to share their works, as well as aiding in the publishing of their books.

I would like to especially thank my husband, Joe Williams, for fostering a home environment that encourages creativity, play, and growth.

I would like to dedicate this book to my sister, Kimberly Helene Edwards, who has been a constant in my life as a mini-mother, deejay, friend, and confidant-*tag*.

Menu

Menu

A
12-course
Buffet
of
Poetry

hors-d'oeuvres

Hors-d'oeuvres introduce the menu prepared

They're the first tempting morsels fit to be shared

The Hunger We All Have

The food for thought prepared here has the goal
of feeding the cravings of your heart and soul
The hunger we all have to connect with others
can be met with this menu, whatever your druthers

When you have no particular appetite
and you search high and low to find the right bite
You scour the pantry, then stare in the fridge
hoping to find that delectable smidge

Something that perfectly hits that spot
Wherever it is, whether you knew where or not
Look no further, helpings are on the way
Read on and you can satiate your pangs today

You can nibble or gnaw, sample and savor
the different courses with their own unique flavor
Herein lies a smorgasbord from which you can nosh
to nourish your brain with some poetic panache

These twelve courses are not a meal per se
Consider these offerings a thought-provoking buffet
Peruse the menu! What sounds tempting? Feel free
to try dessert first!   *¡Bon appétit!*

If My Black Fell Off / Alone in a Room

If my black fell off
What would I be?
Am I black
Or is black me?
Is it my nature
Or my nurture?
Can I foster
What is lost? or
Does my DNA
Dictate the way?

You can take me out of blackness
But not my blackness out of me
I am bound by the roots
Of my ancestral family tree

Yet, my spirit has no color
My soul has no race
When I'm alone in a room,
Who am I in that place?
Does it matter? No one can see me
And for a moment I am free
From the millions of perspectives
That have shaped and molded me

hor-d'oeuvres

Without a mirror who are we?
Without any feedback what could we be?
How would we identify without society?
How would I like to be seen
If I could just be... me?

If my black fell off and I was stripped bare
Alone in a room, with no one to care
I could sit with myself and as if from the womb
See in that quiet what could possibly bloom

Powerful Positive Poetry

The power of positive poetry
invites peers to peer into our know-etry
To produce with a pen and a paper
a parable or a path to a caper
We pretend to be powerful people
Perhaps playing to not appear feeble
Procreating, a pro-creative version
Of a powerful, poetic person
For even the puniest piece of prose pie
Can persuade us to perk up -- poke fear in the eye

Poetry is a powerful positive
That can strengthen a person's prerogative
to challenge one's perspicacity
In particular for those with a piddling voracity
It exercises the muscles that ponder
Perusing a path hither and yonder
Preparing one's spirit for exploration
Purposely fit to forge into a poet's creation
It's the sharing that nurtures and grows
That's the power of positive prose

Positive poetry is powerful
When we recite from our hearts by the hour-ful
as we paint potent pictures with words
and the flights of our minds mimic birds
as we soar to that place, we employ profound choice
To be carried away by that powerful voice
where you see what is said and you feel -- without don't
and you're floating aloft as you will -- without won't
Positively engaged to the utmost degree
'Tis the purpose and power of professed poetry

It can ring a bell that cannot be unrung
it can sing a song that cannot be unsung
It can spin a tale that cannot be unspun
Spoken Word is a deed that cannot be undone

amuse-bouche

This course is to "amuse the mouth" with a
small flavorful taste

Allow these mouthfuls to stimulate your tongue,
read aloud post haste

More or Less

Maybe if I drink more
Then I would care less
It's because I think more
That I have this bare stress

With lessened awareness
I might want to drink more
'Cause life's so unfair yes
And therefore, I'd sink more

A happy, sloppy, open mess
Showing my inner fool more
Without my social finesse
I'd lie upon the cool floor

If I didn't drink more
I'd surely sound dumb less
Perhaps be on the brink more
But feel more than numbness

To the Alphabet

To **A**ging gracefully

To **BE**ing present

To **SEI**zing the day

To **DEE**pening connections

To **EA**sing on down the road

To **EF**forts in effectively communicating that get more
    than 'A's... they get Ahs

To **GE**ometric symmetry

To **H** E double-hockey sticks with conformity

To **I**deas that come to fruition

To **JA**mes Brown and Jane Eyre

To **CA**ke on your birthday

To **EL**evating your standards

To **IM**pacting your surroundings with your best self

To **IN**vesting in yourself

To **O**pening your heart to love

To **PEA**ce on earth

To **CU**te things that make you say 'Awww'

To **AR**t on your inner and outer walls

To **ES**tablishing a healthy life balance

To **TEA**time with scones

To **U**-turns when you need them

To **VE**gan food that tastes good

To **DOUBLE U**se furniture, like a stepstool/table

To **EX**hilarating expeditions

To **WHY** not try

To **ZE**ro regrets

Give Me One

Give me…

One look, one book, one hook, one bad-ass cook

One time, one rhyme, one victimless crime

One kiss, one bliss, one place that I will miss

One he, one she, one who recognizes me

One man, one fan, one who lets me know I can

One day, one way, one who hears what I say

One hope, one nope, one who helps me cope

One hi, one bye, one good reason why

One choice, one voice, one reason to rejoice

One blink, one ink, one truth that makes one think

soup

A good cup of soup can warm your soul

Let these ladle-fuls simmer in your emotional bowl

LABELS

Lumping
All
Beings
Ever-
Lasting
So, don't do it
    Like
    Any-
    Body
    Ever
    Loved a label
    So, consider them fluid
        Labels
        Are for
        Boxes
        Enclosing
        Less inclusive
        So, screw it
            Let's
            All
            Be
            Enablers of
            Love
            So, pursue it
                Leave
                Assumptions
                Behind,
                Evil
                Loses
                    So, get to it!!

Once a Month

I feel sad
Even in my happy lot
I feel alone
Even when I see I'm not
I feel cold
Then in a flash too hot
I feel lost
Found at this very spot

I feel grateful
But still so needy
When I want more
I just feel so greedy
I feel hungry
But know not what will feed me
My life's garden
Seems so weedy

I feel low
And my outlook bleak
I'll see tomorrow
But my attempt is weak
So much is good
It should be that I seek
Where energy flowed like a mighty river
Today there is a dried-up creek

I don't need anyone
We all know that's a lie
I just feel big teary
I need an epic cathartic cry
I will use those tears
To wash beyond the eye
And with my cleansed self
I will get dressed and try

Singleton Woods Reunion

Family Fun
Always Accepting
Meeting Many
Interconnecting In
Living Loving
Years Yo!

Reminiscing
Eating
Uniting
Networking
Interacting
Opening hearts
Naming the faces

There's unity in community
The Singleton-Woods vibe up in this tribe
This re-unity is an opportunity
To bind us like no words can describe

I've got cousins by the dozens
Firsts and seconds once, twice, or three times removed
There are more kinships in these friendships
We are all family as the tree so clearly proved

Birth inserts you into a family
But connections occur when we share the same space
This reunion allows for the ties to bind
We should all cherish the memories we create at this time
and place

Together we are a force
May we never walk alone
Let's refill our familial tanks
With Singleton-Woods-ness home grown!

appetizer

To whet your appetite for the courses to follow

Sample these offerings and feel free to wallow

Your Truth

If your truth seems kind of squishy

And your words are washy wishy

And your story's ever changing

 and the details rearranging

And when you say it's really actual

But it's actually less factual

And you start most things you say

with honestly, for real, really, believe me okay

Then you may not recognize

that we can see though your guise

And the really real that you speak

Doesn't garner the trust that you seek

Movement

My body is a vehicle through which music expresses itself

My movement, my groovement is my nonverbal communication

If you're picking up what I'm putting down while I'm getting down and I'm spinnin' 'round

Then you are in my tribe, up in a vibe that moves us to a better place

Moving slowly or moving fast-ly,

I shake my ass-ets like nobody's watching, but

everybody is

The dance I go into shows how music moves me

The trance I go into thoroughly behooves me

Per chance I'll bump into someone who proves we

connected

I invite you to join me,
shall we move in sync?

       Boyz II Men?
       boy bands
       girl hands
            waving in the air
       my new fans
            jumping out of their chair
       in step, no words
       in complete communion
       a replete reunion

in movement

appetizer

Death

Note: This poem is the product of a challenge issued by my son to write a 10-line piece about Death, using five words, no verbs, no rhymes. Fun fact: This same challenge was given to an AI BOT and it failed.

Breath-
less

Death-
grip

Heart-
ichoke

Under-
ground

Hell-
road

salad

This salad course contains entries

to enrich your health

Consume these verses to

grow your knowledge's wealth

No Feet

There is this 'be thankful' attitude
For those of us in an ungrateful mood
'It could be worse' is meant to add
A perspective that whatever 'it' is, 'it' is less bad

Wallowing in my personal blues
I'd cry because I had no shoes
Until I met a man who had no feet
As problems go, he had me beat

Is he worse off because of his lack?
Or do we have different sets of problems to attack?
We both have issues we need to address
Like I'm trying to reduce my foot-having stress

If we dwell too long on our good fortune and good feet
We won't spend enough time on the challenges we meet
With gratitude we face obstacles to keep out of a hearse
We should hurdle them, not roost on what could be worse

The Wall Changed Me

I came to paint a wall
And the truth came to me
A tattoo on a scar
Where all is washed out to sea

I put paint on this wall
And this wall colored me
It can color us informed
In its vibrance we can see

I learned that there is more to
know
Than any one source can teach
you, so
This mural has connected
stories of
Non-mainstream histories
captured with love

I, a naive girl being all of
sixteen
Heard from a past I had never
seen
Of people who at first didn't
seem like me
But we shared a minority's
familiarity

Before a colorless L.A.
waterway
Now minorities' truths are on
display
From a Tujunga Wash to a great,
mighty Wall
There are lessons and stories to
enlighten us all

The process took a summer
to
Turn blueprints to bluelines
by a motley crew
Of artists and youths with
painted shoes and grit
Atop the magenta wash went
the images that endure, sunlit

She created my brown skin
color with her oranges, yellows,
and greens
And for my buddy, purples, reds
and blues
She didn't use brown paint for
people who looked like us
Our people got our authentic
hues

The multiple colors of my race
Were captured and remain
on this wall
Our people have a
personalized face
A distinct part of us there to
enthrall

I went to work on a wall
And it worked its magic on me
It was just a summer job, or so I thought
But I earned more than money, self-worth can't be bought
I was seen, I was heard, I was valued, I was taught
I learned history, compassion, and that July in the sewer in the valley
is extremely hot

I helped change a wall
And the wall changed me
I am a leaf on the Great Wall of Los Angeles Mural Maker tree
I will always be connected to the people I've met
Both to those working in the trenches and those in this landmark
mural set

Bonds, friendships, knowledge, and pride
To have my eyes now opened wide
To my history along with that of my different-colored kin
Those images depict the similar struggles within
This greatest of countries, the home we all share and know
Has its shames and its scars that through healing together we grow

My name is painted on the Great Wall of LA
When I point it out, my pride carries the day
Three summers... three times in my life I have shined
My people, our spirits forever enshrined

In the universe, I have felt small
As if I'd barely made a ripple at all
But when I speak about the monumental Great Wall
My voice is amplified more than thirteen feet tall

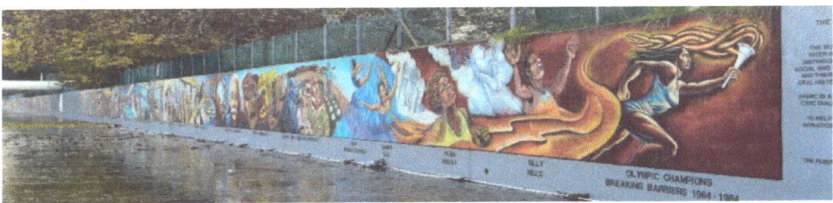

Note: The Great Wall of Los Angeles is a mural painted in the Tujunga Flood
Control Channel in the San Fernando Valley. Judith F Baca, with a team of artists
and youths from the community painted this mural depicting the history of ethnic
peoples of California beginning in prehistoric times. The Great Wall is listed on the
National Register of Historic Places. Pictures (left) Kelly Watts, Priscilla Rouse on
scaffold (above) The Tujunga Wash -- courtesy of greatwallinstitute.sparcinla.org

The Pursuit of Healthiness

Happiness is not easily defined
Which makes it difficult to pursue
But healthiness can be outlined
And consistently attainable too

I am not the first to say
Happiness is a byproduct not a goal
And on any given day
Healthiness will make you more whole

Happiness is overrated
Its aftereffects are often fleeting
Healthiness is understated
But it's what keeps the heart beating

When you achieve healthy
Happiness comes from within
Looking outwardly for happy
Will betray you time and time again

salad

fish

The discourse in this fish course

May be a source you can endorse

The Desire to Feed

The rituals, the festivals, the networks on TV

Celebrate a basic staple of humanity

The power of food and the ceremony of feeding

Bring people together, whatever they're needing

The crunching, the munching, the flavor explosions

The noshes with sauces are magical potions

They can transport us all to nirvana-like places

The pleasures of eating show all over our faces

No matter the race, the culture, the creed

We all have in common the desire to feed

Life in Lies, the Truth

If you live in a lie, where the truth feels intrusive
And the lie feels so good, and the truth more abusive
Then I cannot be your friend, because I live in the real
And the farther you are from it, then the less of you I feel

The truth doesn't hurt if it's through it that you heal
When you let truth be your guide, then before *you* the
world will kneel

If you are a liar, then these words are not for you
However, if you only lie to yourself and to others you are
true
If you want to protect your honor/image and for others
you come through
I entreat you to let your mind on the following chew

If your friend told you they'd bring food at five
And then didn't show up, you'd think they were jive
And if they told you again... five it is
You might give them another chance, but would not trust
as much their biz
Then they don't show, you'd say oh hell no

They are not dependable and now you are wise
These are the folks on whom nobody relies
You cannot believe every word they say
Nor trust them to be true on any given day

…Now let's turn that around…
If you told a friend you'd be there at six
And for this friend, dinner you would fix
You do everything in your power not to disappoint
You'd go superhero-mode to get food to their joint

Because we treat others the way we want to be treated
But, when you tell yourself what you're going to do for
yourself, how is that plan greeted?
You can spot a lie out of others' mouths and deftly know how
to dodge it
But the lie you tell yourself, you let in and cannot seem to
dislodge it

You would never allow a person to treat you the way you
treat yourself
You don't treat others that poorly because you know they'd
put you on the shelf

… The message is…
Live in the truth, that's where true freedom rings
Liberation from the lies can give your spirit wings
If you cannot trust yourself or be sure you'll show up for you
Then how can you expect others to do what you won't do

So … be true!

Touch – Two Ways

Touch (Physical)

When you touch someone
You give a part of yourself
And get someone's something in return
A sensation, a dispensation of the spirit
through the skin
Touch is the most direct way to let whoever
in

Touch (Metaphysical)

Keep in touch
Is said so much
But what does it mean
Once you've left the scene

Let's do lunch
Let's grab drinks
Are the emptiest lines
And nobody thinks
That it will happen
Or they'll see you again
Because if you had meant it
You would have said when

main

The main course is where

the meat of the menu is found

Feast your mind on these poems,

let your imagination be unbound

Bodies Like Buildings – A Sonnet

If we could cherish bodies like buildings
If we could value lives more than luggage
If we used our energy as shieldings
Protection from the slights and the shruggage

If we could see ourselves in our neighbors
If we could be ourselves without a fear
If we could share the fruits of our labors
To nourish humankind as needs appear

If I could be a just human being
If I could just be a seeing human
Get along without always agreeing
And hone my empathetic acumen

We should build others up not tear them down
Let love be an action, not just a noun

Black Enough

Am I not black enough? So, are you?
Are you the standard I should be modeling to?
Have you cornered the market on your race?
Have I finished so far behind first place?
I've been told I'm not black
And no one asked me how that felt
As I sit at life's table
I just play the cards I'm dealt

In high school it was white girls who said I wasn't
black because they liked me
Since I didn't fit the stereotype of those they didn't
like, I could not possibly be
A black friend said I was white (just kidding of course)
But funnily, her 'humor' hit with a blunt force
Is there a culture quiz I didn't pass?
Does it look like I am tryna' pass? Alas!

Instead of changing their definition of a race of
millions of unique individuals
They changed their definition of me
They couldn't color me inside their limited lines
This colored girl has escaped the confines of their
small minds
At last, I am free!

It's not citizenship, there's no passport
Everyone's walk in life is different
And how dare anyone tell anyone else
Who they are
Like they set the bar
And get to tell you how far
You need to go to be a part of a race that has no finish line

I didn't have to fit in, I just went in
Eyes wide open seeing the sights
Accepting the goodness
Deflecting the slights

No matter my vernacular
My blackness is spectacular
I should not be judged on how I talk
But measured more on how I walk
In confidence and easy stride
With intention, mind open wide

To those who think they know
how in my blackness I should live
I am enough and they should know
The little damn I give
I am enough!

Big Old Glasses

*When I'm upset (mostly regarding politics) this is how I talk
about my man on the phone with my girlfriends:*
My man wears big old glasses
But he can't see sh*t
He reads the news every day
But he doesn't know sh*t
He wears his heart on his sleeve
But he can't feel sh*t
He says yes when he hears me talk
But hasn't heard sh*t

*When I'm feeling hyper-analytical/critical this is what I
think:*
He only sees what he's looking for
But there's so much more to be seen
He reads and narrows his point of view
Instead of broadening it and becoming more keen
He has the biggest softest heart
But at times his perception is lean
He hears my words but sometimes just the words
Missing the person and truth in between

Finally, and most of the time - When I see him in his glory
He sees my beauty in ways I cannot
He reads me and adjusts to my too cold, too hot
He gives his heart anew everyday - like yesterday's gift he
forgot
He hears my heartbeat and feeds my needs - so
overfloweth my pot

palate

cleanser

The cleanser course resets your palate for the next

This fare does the job with minimal text

Listen, don't **L**ecture

Ask, don't **A**ssume

Share, don't **S**hutdown

Talk through, don't **T**ip-Toe Around

Strangers

I see how strangers take me in

And think they know me by my skin

But how can any person know

Another without a proper hello?

Ignorance

If ignorance is bliss

then you walk in the world blind

Not caring what you miss

You don't seek so you don't find

second
main

The second main course is gamier than the first

Dive in and let yourself be immersed

This Apple

This apple that is my life
Has had many a worm
Gnawing at its core
Yet there is nurturing flesh
Ready to be consumed
By those seeking sustenance

I still have value after falling from the tree...
That tree with the other apples
in their varying stages of maturity
I am ripe with opportunity
Not afforded those on the tree

For retirement is a road trip
And off the tree, I have hit the road
Seeing sights and uncovering truths
About my peel, my flesh, my seeds, my soul

The truth is life, for as long as I live in it
My core will be preserved
And this apple will maintain its dignity
Even when reduced to sauce

I've been cider, sweet and hard
I've been juice to the thirsty
I will not be found rotten
I am resilient, never forgotten

My Life / The Kelly Williams Show

My life is a musical
and now you have a part
Congratulations to you
for your role in my art
How big will it be?
What scene will we make?
What is the song
into which we will break?

We all are players
on each other's life's stage
And without rehearsal
we've all come of age
There's drama and tragedy
comedy, romance
We cannot know ourselves
lest we endeavor to take a chance

Welcome to my life
for as long as you are near
Come and dance with me as you like
without stage fright or fear
There is no audition
for the Kelly Williams Show
It's playing here right now
Are you ready? Let's go!

I don't take direction
nor respond well to a request
I can follow a good lead
my goal is to bring out our best
This show is on the road
a world tour always in motion
Going with the flow
of this stream or that ocean

The Kelly Williams Show
is not about you, it's about me
When I talk and sing and dance
that's when my true self I see
I play and get to be
or not be what is expected
You can always count on the truth
of my life as I project it

Still, I Rise

Note: This poem was written in response to a Poetry challenge: How has the pandemic changed you? Write a poem inspired by Maya Angelou's poem with the same name. Specifics: First line of the poem must be "still I rise".

Still, I rise
from the gray to the blue
of the skies
as a plane sheds the storm for the calm
it's a balm
Now I know as I rise
that my truth has no disguise
And I'll voice my lessons learned
and my choice is how I churned
and I turned
all my thoughts into verse
as to nurse
the old wounds
felt in this yearlong cocoon

I'm 'bout done not speaking not seeking
Not caring not daring not openly glaring
at the wrong
Going along
for so long I've seemed strong
But I've watched and I've waited
but not openly debated
those who need those who feed
on the meek and the weak

It's my time in this rhyme to be true not just to you
but to me as I see that it's we who can change
rearrange all the fear and the doubt from within and
without into strength for the length of our lives let
us live as we give what we can
as we still rise

cheese

This cheese course is dairy free

If you dare, eat free-ly

Beliefs

Your beliefs are yours alone
and them you are entitled to
Does that mean that the world
must believe the same things you do?

If you show me something I cannot see
does that make something wrong with you or with me?

The answer is neither
It's not wrong versus right
We're not solely good or bad
Nothing's simply black and white

Your truths are not global
They are as personal as you can get
So why expect universal agreement
from people you've not met

When someone believes something
that to you cannot ring true
It won't be intensity nor persistent passion
that will turn the tide for you

We must accept that we can all live together in peace
If we give others the same due respect we expect
regarding our choices, our lives
and most assuredly our beliefs

It's a Choice

We like whom we like
and we don't whom we don't
We do not get to choose
whom we will or whom we won't

We do however
choose whom we hate
It is truly a choice
and the consequences great

Not the good great
but profound in magnitude and effect
To hate those you do not know
takes a blind commitment to disrespect

Love Grammar

In diagramming a sentence, we find the subject, the verb, and the object or the predicate.

In the sentence 'I love you', 'love' is the verb.

A verb is an action word, so if you love someone, that someone should feel it.

Instead of 'I love you', some should more accurately state 'I have love for you',

Then it's all about the speaker.

It's more authentic and definitely not about 'you' receiving the noun 'love',

Unless the subject decides to make you the object of the transitive verb, 'love'.

dessert

This course includes sweetness and words to delight

to bring smiles to your mouth with every bite

Thank You

Thank you is the card that always plays

From whatever hand your situation dealt

Whatever information you have received

Be grateful and tuck it into your belt

Knowledge is power to wield at will

It is neither good nor bad

It's required to navigate situations

Without it you'd drive yourself mad

There is no useless knowledge

Information is much needed data

It's what you do with the facts

That makes you a lover or a hate-a

Ode to Apple Pie

This a shout out to apple pie
My dessert boo, my chew or die
From the cinny-cinnamon to the nutty-nutmeg
To the flick-flakiest crust
On my knees I would beg

For a pièce de résistance
Be it baked or be it fried
Even if it be frozen
No apple pie will be untried

How about them apples
And how their crispness makes me feel
There's a neatness to their sweetness
I need to get them outta their peel

Then I mix them with the spices
Spoon that on a freshly rolled crust
Add a lattice top for beauty
Made from scratch is such a must

Then I pop it in the oven
And the smell arouses me
That aroma, I am lovin'
Is that bubbling I see?

When raw apples become filling
The mix has reached full piehood
Titillating my senses full tilt
I breathe in all the pie good

Oh, the patience that it takes
To let the pie cool to perfection
Debating straight up or a la mode
What will be today's predilection?

The rolling, the mixing
The peeling, the fixing
The baking, the flaking
The whole undertaking

Apple pie, how I love you
Even after you're eaten and gone
You must know I'll make another
So that your spirit will live on!

The Color of His Love

I married a man who doesn't look like me
And for some folks that is all they can see
I wish for them that they could know
The color of his love, his light, his glow

Why did I marry a man of a different color?
I've often thought about a proper response to a question
that is nobody's business, but my own

Here and now, I will state the obvious…

It is not because of the color of his skin
It's because of the color of his love
It's not white nor black
But feels like the spectrum of a rainbow across my heart
as big as the sky with no end

The color of his love is warm and deep and rich and
soothing
It radiates and resonates in my inner core
The color lights me up and calms me down
So I can rest and restore my faith in big and colorful love

I'm finally living in color, after a black and white life

No one who has seen him look at me asks that question
Because what is clearly visible to anyone looking is the
beaming color of his love

mignardise

Last but not least is the course mignardise

With treats meant to be relished with ease

Go to Bed

Go to bed I said to myself
But I lacked conviction
Why should I? was my reply
With a hint of contradiction
Like you don't know
must we engage in this nightly friction
Although tired,
Sleep seems an undesired constriction

It's about being defiant, noncompliant,
Anti-establishment of the bedtime norm
To not always acquiesce to the laws of my body's nature
To not do right and conform
To exert free will with my ultimate power
To rage against the nonexistent storm
To feel the chill of midnight naked
Then to compel myself toward the warm

I love the endless quiet of night
When everyone is down and retired
The quintessential me-time
When all things are possible, but none are required
To sit with myself and hear my mind
roam around the world unmired
'Twas on a night precisely like this
that a poem was inspired

I Am an African Daisy

I am an African Daisy, one of my favorite flowers. How do I know? I will walk you through the evidence:

1. An African Daisy is a beautiful flower; an African American Kelly is a beautiful flower

2. It has multiple varieties; I have multiple varieties (i.e. moods)

3. It represents Purity and Innocence; I represent Purity that is the result of refinement (i.e. removal of impurities) derived from Maturity, and I'm always assumed guilty, though I usually prove my Innocence

4. African Daisies have a good shape and can form a dramatic display of color; I am in good shape and can put on a dramatic display, thanks to my color

5. They are attractive; Kelly is…, do I have to say it?!

6. African Daisies come in numerous colors and shades including blue, purple, mauve, pink, yellow, and cream; Kelly comes in lots of shades of brown (depending on the season), but I do come in looking good wearing blue, purple, mauve, pink, yellow, and cream

7. They do not appear to be fussy about soil pH; I do not appear to be fussy about soil pH

8. African Daisies are low maintenance; I am low maintenance (don't ask my husband)

9. They are sun-loving; I am son-loving... and daughter-loving!

10. African Daisies have increased in popularity; I too have increased in popularity as I continue to open my petals/art to the world!

The Retirement Requirement

The question: What are you going to do?
My answer: It's what I'm not going to do!

Retirement...
I realized my life has been uncovered
Like furniture sitting in storage
I knew it was there, but really didn't give it notice
Because it didn't fit into my current situation
And I had no time to sit

My time of reckoning has come, and I now know
that working at a job was just a distraction from the
life I kept saying I would live "If I had the time"

So now... I have time and oh wow
I am lost and found in it
I'm trying to find my footing and discover
Where exactly I'm trying to go and
Who exactly I'm trying to be and
How exactly I'm going to get there
And why exactly do I keep saying exactly?
This is exactly what freedom is not
There is no exactness in exploration
No precision in the path to the self
There is no recipe inside a book sitting upon some
shelf

The retirement requirement is to be free and
spontaneous and open and willing to sit without a plan
and let your day, yourself, your life unfold

Each night when you "retire" to your bed do you
reflect
upon your where, your who, your how, and ultimately
your life with due respect?

The End

The Beginning...

mignardise

extras:
Chef Kelly's
Grab-N-Go
Word Salads

Behold these bonus one of-a-kind take-away treats

Concoctions made from random selections

are surprisingly good eats

Word Salad #1 - Goldilocks Is a Karen

Salad Challenge #1:
  Use the following ten ingredients in a piece from the antagonist's point-of-view from a well-known story

Salad Ingredients:
  1. Crawl
  2. Wild
  3. Muscle/Mussel
  4. List
  5. Balloon

  6. Skitter
  7. Front
  8. Type of nuts
  9. Use a simile
  10. Type of condiment

 ## *Goldilocks is a Karen*

Hi! I'm a Karen. Cut! Keep going? Hi, I'm Karen, a.k.a. Goldilocks and I want to start by saying "Bear Lives Matter"! I'm here to clear the air and set the record straight. I mean, I am not the antagonist in my recent bear encounter. There have been many wild accusations about me and this situation has ballooned into a horrific tale, with a laundry-list of wrongdoings on my part. As if I would ever muscle my way into a bear's home.

Here's what really happened:
I was out walking, minding my own business when my nose was assaulted by the most delicious aroma wafting from a window (quick note to bears and anyone really: If you don't want people coming into your house and eating your porridge, don't leave your window open and have it smell soooo good! OMG). Anywho, it's not like I crawled through the window! I walked through the front door. I mean, the mat said WELCOME!

When I saw those bowls on the table, it was like an invitation. So, I added some of the sugar and honey (those bears do think of everything) and it was just… "right"! Then just… wrong! There must have been walnuts, or pistachios, or hazelnuts, peanuts, or gluten in that porridge because I started having a severe allergic reaction. I may have broken a chair or two as I skitter-scattered around the house looking for allergy medicine. But I was the victim here! I could have died! Luckily, I found some Benadryl just in time, downed the bottle, and immediately felt exhausted. I was as tired as an 18-wheeler (now that's really tired)! So, I took a nap!

As anyone can clearly see, this has been a big misunderstanding, not a B&E! I wish Papa, Mama, and Baby Bear all the best and they can rest assured that I will not be pursuing any legal action regarding my near-death experience in their home.

Bears, I forgive you!

Also, would you please DM me that porridge recipe? It is killer!

Word Salad #2 – Strange Bird

Salad Challenge #2:

Create a piece using the following ten ingredients, NOT about yourself, but where the first letter of each line spells your name in acrostic fashion

Salad Ingredients:

1. Blur
2. Abnormal
3. Sign/Sine
4. Sleep
5. Type of flower/flour
6. Flinch
7. Frost
8. Fudge
9. Puzzle
10. One of the seven wonders of the world (ancient or modern)

Strange Bird

Keeping an unflinching watch over the valley below
Eyes unblinking, as vigilant as the Sphinx himself
Looming regally in both the frost and heat
Larger than life
You stand (or is that some abnormal crouch?) your ground

Without
A way
To get closer
To you, I puzzle and marvel at how you
Seem perfectly balanced, situated upon your perch

Who is this strange sleepless bird? As
I blur my vision for a clearer view, you
Look
Like an immovable guardian
In the distance, with the calm and peace of a lily
Atop the highest peak,
More like a sculpture, with wind-coaxed
Signs of life, than the actual pile of rocks that nature or
                                        man fudged into existence

Word Salad #3 #4 #5 –
Dinner, Breakfast, Lunch

Three-way Salad Challenge #3, #4, #5:
Inter-connect the next three sets of ten ingredients into a common theme

Dinner (Salad #3) Ingredients:

1. Weary
2. Volcano
3. Poke
4. Burrow
5. Mangle
6. Bowl
7. Cascade
8. Surrender
9. Mirror
10. Jumble

Breakfast (Salad #4) Ingredients:

1. Ring
2. Shrug
3. Drape
4. Dangle
5. Prowl
6. Applause
7. Collapse
8. Pour
9. Eye
10. Gorge

Lunch (Salad #5) Ingredients:

1. Wool
2. Bridge
3. Drone
4. Squirm
5. Reject
6. Fingerprint
7. Bruise
8. Claw
9. Puddle
10. Falter

Dinner… A Bowl and a Roll

Firstly, I surrender to the jumble that is a Poke Bowl.
I burrow my fork into the mangled mess I've made, after several weary attempts to grab the fish, rice, and vegetables with chopsticks.
Secondly, a cascade of low-sodium soy sauce hits my wasabi, mirroring a waterfall hitting the rocks below, creating the perfect dip for my Volcano Roll!

Breakfast of Champions

After being on the prowl in the pantry and fridge to find something to gorge on to satiate the cravings for an applause-worthy breakfast but nothing rings tasty, I collapse at the breakfast bar, awaiting inspiration.
My feet dangle from the barstool as I try to shrug off the feeling that, while I want to create a magical meal draped in the culinary secrets of Iron Chefs, I will ultimately pour myself a bowl of the Honey Nut Cheerios I eye-balled when I walked in.

Lunch with a Soon-to-be Ex-Friend

As I sit across the table from her, I start to internally squirm and hope I do not falter in my attempt to end a sometimes-toxic friendship.
My truth will definitely bruise the ego of this semi-narcissist who makes me feel uncomfortable, like when I wear wool to which I am allergic.
I have decided to burn this bridge.
I reject continuing to wallow in her small and lacking puddle of companionship, no longer wondering why she couldn't be there for me.
I won't drone on about what's wrong, just nimbly claw my way out of this entanglement and exit this lunch and "friendship" without leaving so much as a fingerprint behind.

Word Salad #6 - Did You Know?
A Letter to My Mom

Salad Challenge #6:
Write a poem consisting entirely of questions (suggestion is to have 21 in total)

Salad Ingredients:

1. Spine
2. Comedy
3. A psychological term
4. Geranium
5. A noun used as a verb
6. Remedy
7. Name of a town
8. Lift
9. Reticent
10. A phrase in a foreign language

Did You Know? A Letter to My Mom

1. Why is it so hard to write this letter to you?

2. Why am I so reticent to show you who I am?

3. Is it because I am afraid of your scrutiny, even in your death?

4. Is this letter a remedy for all of my childhood trauma I associate with you?

5. Or, is my truth like a geranium, aesthetically good-looking, but stinky so please don't bring it in the house?

6. Were you happy when I was born that June night in Rantoul, IL?

7. Or did the joy come in knowing that I would be the last?

8. Did me Caesarian-sectioning you make me a heroine or just live baby #6 that deactivated your womb when I brought part of it into the world with me?

9. Why didn't you tell me I was baptized on that very day in the incubator because my heart was so weak?

10. Did you know I didn't know I had a middle name until Kim told me as I was practicing writing my name for the first day of kindergarten?

11. Did you know I learned to close my eyes to go to sleep from Carol Brady, because I don't recall being tucked in at night by my non-TV mom?

12. Did you know how self-conscious I was about my full lips because you told me to hold them in?

13. Did you know that I now see that your childhood trauma made it difficult for you to trust anyone?

14. Do you remember all the times we sang songs like "Que Sera, Sera", and made up a dance to "Everyday People"?

15. Can I posthumously thank you for raising me to have a strong spine, to be independent and capable?

16. Did you know I find comedy in every day because that's what you did?

17. Did you know I mastered from scratch pie-crusts, after watching you cuss and struggle with them every Thanksgiving?

18. Do you know that one of my favorite memories with you was when we went to the UCLA/USC game, and UCLA won in the final minute, and on the bumper-to-bumper freeway going home, I shook my UCLA pom-pom out the window, and as far as I could see, all the cars around us did the same?

19. Did you know my favorite place to be is a nursery, because you would always take me when you went?

20. Did you know that I only truly saw your un-edited love for me when Alzheimer's lifted the once impenetrable dome of protection surrounding your heart?

21. Will you forgive me for not recognizing it sooner?

Word Salad #7 - Suddenly Spring Strikes the Senses

Salad Challenge #7:
Use any one of the lines, except the first, from Jack Gilbert's poem "Horses at Midnight Without a Moon" as your own first line

Salad Ingredients:
1. Soil
2. Web
3. Kite
4. Point
5. Sour
6. Bare/Bear/Fair/Fare
7. Sequester
8. Fashion
9. Type of bread
10. Type of glassware

Extra challenge ingredient: Discombobulate

Suddenly Spring Strikes the Senses

Who suddenly smells flowers**
Springing from the soil
Dancing in the fashion of a kite on a string?

Who suddenly feels discombobulated
When the sun hits you full-on, point blank
Revealing all that artificial light does not?

Who suddenly hears the rain
Drops caught in spider webs
In the sequester of a tree's hollow?

Who suddenly tastes the delights of mother nature
Breathing in the aromas of the sweet woods and sour
grasses
Drinking in the mist from her plentifully bedewed chalice?

Who suddenly sees the rainbow
Baring it's fair beauty across the sky
As comforting to the spirit as biscuits and gravy are to the
soul?

**From *Jack Gilbert's poem "Horses at Midnight Without a Moon"*

Word Salad #8 - da' Bears

Salad Challenge #8:
Write about your spirit animal

Salad Ingredients:
1. Burden
2. Foot
3. Cozy
4. Blast
5. Cling
6. Air
7. Roof
8. Nature
9. Type of soup
10. Type of grain

da' Bears

I can barely remember when I didn't feel like a bear
Barefoot and playful with nary a care
And I do love a cozy hibernation
under a snow-covered roof sleeping is liberation
from the daily burden of finding something to eat
And there's the reduction of time on my bear-feet
Like gumbo with rice, we are rich in our makeup
we cling to our peace when we finally do wake up

People aren't likely to poke bears because
of our presence and strength and our super sharp claws
We enjoy tree-climbing, salmon fishing, and bothering bees
for their honey
Sliding on snow in crisp arctic air or romping in nature
whenever it's sunny

There's Fozzy, Fuzzy Wuzzy, Paddington, and Pooh
Smokey, Teddy, Yogi and his associate, Boo Boo
Pandas and Polars and Grizzlies oh my
Black and Brown bears, Sloth and Spectacled bears, Sun and
Moon bears, no lie

Found on four continents, in various colors and sizes
Getting to know us bears takes more than anyone surmises
Whether in a blast of winter chill or in a gentle summer
breeze
We survive and we thrive wherever we please

Lastly, we are entirely opposed to a bearskin rug
We are attire-ly disposed to a bare skin hug!
'Cause hugs are quintessentially a bear thing to do
Bare-naked or not is altogether up to you!

Word Salad #9 - Sighs Matter

Salad Challenge #9:

After reading Ted Kooser's poem "The Sigh," write your own "sigh" piece. Try to make it nine lines like Kooser's.

Salad Ingredients:

1. Grave
2. Crochet
3. Search
4. Tempt
5. Skin
6. Puzzle
7. A color
8. Tool a blacksmith uses
9. A natural ingredient
10. A type of illness

Extra challenge ingredient: Collagen

I *sigh* as I listen to Si(gh)mon and Garfunkel's The Sound of Si(gh)lence

I'm tempted to *sigh* me a river as I search for what is like collagen to the skin

A boost, a filler to help me feel fuller from within, a something I can project to the outsi(gh)de

Should I take a hammer to myself, a wrong-si(gh)zed and ill-shaped puzzle piece to make me fit?

Shall I have their social norms crocheted into my psy(gh)che, intricately interwoven, seams out of *sigh*t?

A patchwork of inauthentic bio-rhythms and blues to move and color me

As remote as Si(gh)beria, as deadly as an uncommon cold, as grave as a si(gh)lent night

My insi(gh)de voice incessantly speaks volumes into the up and down cy(gh)cles of my self-doubt

Sigh-day, the one between Thursday and Saturday, is the day I lick the salt from the wounds soci(gh)ety has inflicted on my delicate Psy(gh)chedelic self

Word Salad #10 - When You Doubt the World

Salad Challenge #10:

Write a "when you doubt the world" poem using the first line of Nathalie Handal's poem "Accepting Heaven at Great Basin" which begins "When you doubt the world...."

Salad Ingredients:

1. Cling
2. Bump
3. Switch
4. Type of musical group
5. Watch
6. Sashay
7. A dessert
8. Embroider
9. Revolution
10. A geographical word

Extra challenge ingredient: Stigmatize

When You Doubt the World

When you doubt the world
Stop watching embroidered tales on TV
When you let in the silence
In the quiet you'll see you're free

From the outside world
And it's unnavigable terrain
You can finally get to play
Around in your curious brain

For there is so much to question
So many trains of thought to catch
In exploration is the best fun
So many pumpkins in your life's patch

Switch from input to output
Let your thoughts sashay about
Let them bump into the others
Let each one jump up and shout

When you doubt the world
More than a second hand's revolution
Be a cobbler of the truth
And filter out the word pollution

Let go of second-hand "knowledge"
Don't join the chorus of fake views
Rebel against blindly following
Those who misrepresent the news

When we stigmatize the truth
The world does become doubtable
But we can cling to the belief
That our inside light is out-able

Word Salad #11 –
In the Old Age Black Was Not Counted Fair

Salad Challenge #11:
Write a sonnet using the first line of one of Shakespeare's sonnets as your title. Maybe that title even acts as a first line.

Salad Ingredients:
1. Limp
2. Morsel
3. Skin
4. Presumptuous
5. Embrace
6. July
7. Beauty
8. Dazzle
9. Prom
10. Something from the 80's

Extra challenge ingredient: Name an Indigenous People

In the Old Age Black Was Not Counted Fair

In the old age black was not counted fair**
But this July after the torch is lit
Skill, not skin is the judged morsel to bear
With medals awarded to those most fit

1904 George Poage started the list
Then Jesse and Wilma earning their golds
In '68, Smith with a lifted fist
Showed a black power the wide world beholds

Olympics have no presumptuousness
Representing your country and your race
Sac-Fox Jim Thorpe was too considered less
Then his gold earned him his country's embrace

Of late, the dazzling beauty, limping Biles
Her promenade sprinkled with neon smiles

**From William Shakespeare's sonnet #127*

Word Salad #12 - Medusa, the Musical

Salad Challenge #12:
Create a piece using the following ten ingredients that includes a mythical or folklore creature

Salad Ingredients:

1. Lizard
2. Fake
3. Air
4. A type of coffee
5. Kitchen
6. Bridge
7. Bristle
8. Socks
9. Green
10. Reference to Winter

 ## Medusa, the Musical

Dressing suggestion: Sing loosely to the tune of "Part of Your World" from The Little Mermaid

Look at these stones
Some'd say they're neat
This one was Roger
And that one was Pete
Wouldn't you think Wow!
These still-life's look so serene

Snakes are my hair
They give me the air
Of a stone-cold monster
But don't you dare stare
But how can you not take a peek
At my skin that's glowing so green

I've turned lizards in blizzards to pet rocks
My only friends are connected to me
In their socks, I have frozen all those when
They've dropped by for iced coffee or tea

I want to be where the people are
Making eye contact with no one dying
Getting whistles not bristles, when I walk down the street

Petrifying your friends doesn't get you far
Wearing dark glasses only hides your crying
When your people are pebbles, your world is concrete

I'd hide under a bridge for a smidge just to be near the action
In the kitchen I'd stay though I'm itchin' to play where it
doesn't lack sun
I'd like to smile at guy and that guy not go dry as a statue
Oh, this curse is the worst when all I can do is dispatch you

I want to show what's behind the glow
It'd be amazing when at me you're gazing
I would rock your world not death but, to life

Betcha I'd make
friends who aren't fake
Betcha they'd truly
get to know me
And they'd treat me with kindness
within their blindness
We'd get to unravel
what's beneath the gravel

If there were a chance
With a glance at a dance
That I could have more than a stone to romance
But how could that be with someone like me?

I'm ready to wink
And with one magic blink
Sneakily slink these snakes down the sink
Ready to be someone to see
A non-lethal rock star part of the world!

entertain-
mints

Video delights for you to savor

Relish in the Spoken Word flavor

Assorted Dishes of Entertain-mints
(Scannable QR Codes)

Big Old Glasses – pg. 38

Black Enough – pg. 36

Bodies Like Buildings – pg. 35

da' Bears – pg. 78

Give Me One – pg. 11

entertain-mints

entertain-mints

www.ingramcontent.com/pod-product-compliance
Lightning Source LLC
Chambersburg PA
CBHW040904120626
46551CB00006B/635